NATURE HEALS

GARDENING IN NATURE

BY ABBY COLICH

BLUE OWL
BOOKS

TIPS FOR CAREGIVERS

Social and emotional learning (SEL) helps children manage emotions, learn how to feel empathy, create and achieve goals, and make good decisions. One goal of teaching SEL skills is to help children care for themselves, others, and the world around them. The more time children spend in nature and the more they learn about it, the more likely they will be to appreciate it and receive its emotional benefits.

BEFORE READING

Talk to the reader about any experience he or she has gardening or taking care of plants.

Discuss: Have you grown plants in the past? What supplies do you need to grow and take care of them? What do plants need to survive?

AFTER READING

Talk to the reader about the benefits of gardening and taking care of plants.

Discuss: What can you learn from gardening? How can gardening make you feel more connected to nature? How can gardening help you be more mindful?

SEL GOAL

Children may struggle with processing their emotions, and they may lack accessible tools to help them do so. Explain to children that nature can help people feel good. Gardening can help us learn patience, responsibility, and respect for nature. Inspire children to learn more about gardening by explaining the many benefits the activity can provide. Whether growing fruits and vegetables to eat, planting flowers, or joining a community garden, gardening offers many ways to connect with nature and yourself.

TABLE OF CONTENTS

CHAPTER 1

WHY GARDEN?

If you had a garden, what would you grow? You can grow flowers, **herbs**, fruits, and vegetables in gardens. Gardens can be large or small.

herbs

Plan out your garden! Doing this can help you use your **imagination** and **creativity**. What specific kinds of flowers, herbs, fruits, or vegetables will you plant? How will you organize them?

Gardening teaches **mindfulness** and so much more. It can help you **focus** on what you are doing in the moment. You may worry less about what bothers you. Taking care of your garden will help you learn **responsibility**. Waiting for plants to grow teaches **patience**.

GOOD FOR YOUR MIND

Studies show that just spending time in a garden or around plants can improve your mood and lower **stress**. It can even improve your memory!

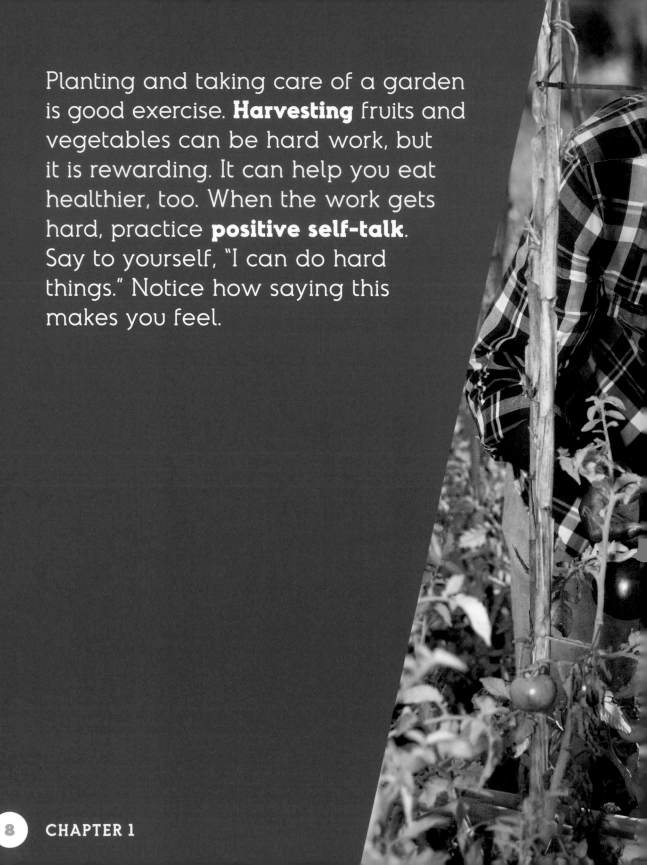

Planting and taking care of a garden is good exercise. **Harvesting** fruits and vegetables can be hard work, but it is rewarding. It can help you eat healthier, too. When the work gets hard, practice **positive self-talk**. Say to yourself, "I can do hard things." Notice how saying this makes you feel.

CHAPTER 2

KNOW BEFORE YOU GROW

Have an adult help you find information about the plants that grow well where you live. Find out what time of year is best to start your garden. Then find the best spot. You can use the ground or containers. Make sure your plants will have enough space and sunlight.

If you plant in containers, you will need soil. Tools like a trowel or rake will make planting easier. Don't forget a watering can or hose!

◀····· **trowel**

community garden

If you don't have space for a garden where you live, you might be able to share a space with others. An adult can help you look for a **community garden** in your area. Or try growing plants indoors. Just make sure they have enough space, sunlight, and water.

CHAPTER 3

MINDFUL GARDENING

Once you have your supplies and your space, it is time to plant! First, smooth out your soil. Break up any clumps. Pay attention to how the soil feels in your hands.

soil

seedling

When you plant your seeds or **seedlings**, be gentle. Make sure each plant will have enough space to grow. Think about ways in which you want to grow, too. Do you want to learn to be more patient? Or maybe you want to focus better in school. What other ways can you grow?

Take care of your garden. Check on it often. Checking on and watching your plants' growth can help you be more **observant** and patient.

Pull out any weeds. As you pull them, imagine they are negative thoughts you are pulling from your mind.

KEEP TRACK

Make a chart to keep track of when you water your garden. Be sure to mark when it rains. You probably won't need to water on rainy days. Check the soil to see if it needs more water.

stem

roots

Imagine you are a plant. A plant's stem and leaves grow tall. Its roots grow down into the ground. Plants stay strong during all sorts of weather. In what ways are you strong like a plant?

KEEP GROWING!

Plants may die before they **bloom**. Don't give up! Try to figure out what went wrong. Maybe your plants had too much sun or too much water. Learn from your mistakes and try again.

Gardening is hard work, but it can be very rewarding. Enjoy it! Take time to feel proud of your work. Spend time **meditating** in your garden or just calming your mind. Find a place to sit up straight. Close your eyes and breathe deeply for a few moments. How do you feel?

GOALS AND TOOLS

GROW WITH GOALS

As the plants in your garden grow, your mind will, too. Practice these goals to help learn responsibility, planning, and patience.

Goal: Start a plant journal. Draw a picture of a young plant from your garden, yard, or neighborhood. Draw it each day as it grows. How does it change over time?

Goal: Go on a mindfulness plant walk. Walk around your neighborhood, a park, or a flower garden. Focus on all the different plants you see, including trees, bushes, grass, and flowers. How do you feel?

Goal: Research a plant that you want to know more about. What kind of care does it need? Could you grow it in your area?

MINDFULNESS EXERCISE

Find a quiet spot. Place your feet slightly apart on the ground. Stand up straight and tall. Close your eyes. Slowly breathe in and out. Imagine you are a plant. Imagine roots growing down from your feet and into the ground. Imagine your legs and torso are a stem, standing straight and tall. Picture your arms as leaves. Continue to breathe in and out for a few minutes. Then open your eyes. Do you feel differently now?

GLOSSARY

bloom
To produce flowers.

community garden
A piece of land that is gardened by a group of people.

creativity
The ability to make new things or think of new ideas.

focus
To concentrate on something.

harvesting
Gathering a crop.

herbs
Plants used to season foods.

imagination
The ability to think of new things.

meditating
Thinking deeply and quietly as a way of relaxing your mind and body.

mindfulness
A mentality achieved by focusing on the present moment and calmly recognizing and accepting your feelings, thoughts, and sensations.

observant
Alert or good at noticing what is going on around you.

patience
The ability to put up with problems or delays without getting angry or upset.

positive self-talk
Words or thoughts to yourself that make you feel good about yourself and your abilities.

responsibility
A duty or job.

seedlings
Young plants.

stress
Mental or emotional strain or pressure.

TO LEARN MORE

FACT SURFER

Finding more information is as easy as 1, 2, 3.

1. Go to www.factsurfer.com

2. Enter "**gardeninginnature**" into the search box.

3. Choose your book to see a list of websites.

INDEX

Blue Owl Books are published by Jump!, 5357 Penn Avenue South, Minneapolis, MN 55419, www.jumplibrary.com

Copyright © 2021 Jump! International copyright reserved in all countries. No part of this book may be reproduced in any form without written permission from the publisher.

Library of Congress Cataloging-in-Publication Data

Names: Colich, Abby, author.
Title: Gardening in nature / by Abby Colich.
Description: Minneapolis: Jump!, Inc., 2021.
Series: Nature heals | Includes index. | Audience: Ages 7–10
Identifiers: LCCN 2020036265 (print)
LCCN 2020036266 (ebook)
ISBN 9781645278375 (hardcover)
ISBN 9781645278382 (paperback)
ISBN 9781645278399 (ebook)
Subjects: LCSH: Gardening–Juvenile literature. | Gardening–Therapeutic use–Juvenile literature. | Mindfulness (Psychology)–Juvenile literature.
Classification: LCC SB457 .C65 2021 (print) | LCC SB457 (ebook)
DDC 615.8/515–dc23
LC record available at https://lccn.loc.gov/2020036265
LC ebook record available at https://lccn.loc.gov/2020036266

Editor: Eliza Leahy
Designer: Michelle Sonnek

Photo Credits: Valery Evlakhov/Shutterstock, cover; sevenke/Shutterstock, 1 (background); Andreja Donko/Shutterstock, 1 (foreground); Anna Klepatckaya/Shutterstock, 3; Ivonne Wierink/Shutterstock, 4 (left); iStock, 4 (right); Oleg Troino/Shutterstock, 5; AnnGaysorn/Shutterstock, 6–7; Iakov Filimonov/Shutterstock, 8–9; Creativa Images/Shutterstock, 10; Alexander Raths/Shutterstock, 11; SolStock/iStock, 12–13; yevgeniy11/Shutterstock, 14 (background); giedre vaitekune/Shutterstock, 14 (foreground); Singkham/Shutterstock, 15; Andrey Sayfutdinov/Shutterstock, 16–17; ThomasVogel/iStock, 18–19; sutlafk/Shutterstock, 20–21.

Printed in the United States of America at Corporate Graphics in North Mankato, Minnesota.